Colourful Coral

Written by Bronwyn Tainui

Illustrated by Omar Aranda

Flying Start
to Literacy®

T0363459

Contents

Chapter 1
Arriving

"Wake up, sleepyhead! We are here!" said Dad as he plopped Bianca down on the sofa. Bianca opened her eyes and blinked. A circle of smiling faces looked down at her.

"Hello Bianca! We're so excited you're here! I am your cousin Maria." A young woman with long, wavy hair opened her arms wide. Bianca knew Maria's face from all the photos she'd seen over the years, but Maria was even lovelier in person.

Bianca had been waiting for this day for a long time. Now, here she was with cousins, aunties and uncles, all talking at the same time. She was back in the place where her mother had once lived. She and her dad were visiting for one week. Not only were they meeting Bianca's mum's family, but they were going to dive on the coral reef for the first time.

"You have travelled all this way to visit us," said Aunt Rosa. "You must be hungry."

Bianca felt happy as she and her dad sat around the big family table with the others. It wasn't that she was unhappy when it was just Dad and her, but this was different.

Bianca's mum had died in a car accident when she was four years old. She could remember only little things about her mother, like a song her mum sang and the way she smelled of flowers. And, because Bianca's dad worked such long hours, Bianca often felt lonely.

But now, surrounded by her mum's family, memories of her mum came flooding back to Bianca. Feeling embraced by her whole family gave Bianca a warm glow inside. Their smiling faces told her, "Welcome home, Bianca. You belong here."

Chapter 2

Dad and Bianca

It had been just Bianca and her dad for most of Bianca's life. They lived in Auckland, New Zealand, in an apartment above one of Dad's restaurants. Dad was always busy, and he couldn't spend a lot of time with Bianca.

When she wasn't at school, Bianca often settled in at the restaurant below the apartment. There was a little table reserved for her beside the aquarium. Bianca sat there, pretending to do homework, but usually she was drawing the vibrant butterflyfish. Dad would frown when he saw Bianca drawing.

"I want you to study maths and English, subjects that will help you in life," Dad said.

"Art makes me happy," Bianca replied.

Bianca had a sinking feeling that Dad would never understand.

One day, as Bianca sat staring at the butterflyfish, she was taken into another world – their world. She began to look at photos of butterflyfish online, and she saw scuba divers swimming with the fish in the coral reefs. If only she could join them . . .

"I want to go scuba diving at the coral reefs with the butterflyfish," Bianca told Dad at breakfast one morning.

He looked up. "Your cousins in Australia often go out diving. Your cousin Maria is a marine biologist."

"We're going to visit them next year," Bianca reminded him. "Can I go diving with my cousins?"

Dad looked thoughtful. "Diving is an adult sport," he said. "But it could be good for both of us to learn how to dive. You would have to do as you are told."

Dad smiled his special smile and Bianca got excited. *My dream might turn into reality!* she thought.

A few weeks later, Bianca discovered how much work learning to dive involved.

"You are nearly twelve, Bianca," the diving instructor said. "If you are mature for your age, that's old enough to get your Junior Open Water Diver Certificate. Are you good at following instructions?"

Dad looked at Bianca as she nodded. They both knew that was not always true.

First, Bianca and Dad had to read the diving manual. Sometimes Bianca had a problem staying focused. But Dad took her hand and said, "Bianca, together we can do this." And, working together, they did.

A month later, they both felt confident that all this information had finally been absorbed. They knew how to care for their diving equipment, how to manage buoyancy and much more. They practised the hand signals for communicating with a diving buddy. The buddy system was very important for safe diving.

At their first session in the shallow end of the pool, Bianca tried her best to control her excitement and listen to the instructor. Under the water, Bianca began to breathe through her mouthpiece and saw the first bubbles float upwards. It felt strange to be breathing freely underwater, but Bianca loved the experience, even in the pool. And it got better with each session when they started diving in the ocean.

On the last day of their practical diving training, Bianca and her dad were going to dive off a boat in open water. At breakfast, Dad and Bianca looked at the site map.

"We'll be diving to eight metres, and we will be able to have a good look around," said Dad.

This was the day Bianca hoped to get her Junior Open Water Diver Certificate. She was so nervous.

"Don't worry," said Dad. "You will pass."

"I hope so," Bianca replied.

Bianca followed the diving instructor off the side of the boat. She stayed with Dad, who was her diving buddy, but it felt like she was in her own world down there in the deep, quiet water.

"Congratulations, Bianca," said the diving instructor as she handed Bianca her Junior Open Water Diver Certificate. Both Bianca and her dad held up their diver certificates and took a selfie. They could not stop smiling.

I am ready for diving on the Great Barrier Reef! thought Bianca.

Chapter 3
Paradise bleached

"Can we go diving today?" Bianca asked Maria.

"You can come diving with me and my team, but we're working," said Maria. She looked serious. "There's been a lot of bleaching of the coral this summer. I'm afraid it won't be the colourful underwater experience you'd hoped for."

Bianca knew what "bleaching" meant. She'd read about this online. The multicoloured coral, home to thousands of fish and other forms of marine life, turns white and often dies.

"Is this because of climate change?" Bianca asked her cousin.

"That's a big part of the problem, for sure," Maria said. "But the coral is facing other threats, too. Much of our coral is now infected with a disease called white syndrome. It's causing white patches and rings on the coral."

Maria looked at Bianca's sad face.

"This is serious, but we have to stay positive and keep working. The coral reef took hundreds of years to form. The team is monitoring the changes. We're diving every day and photographing what we see. The more we know, the better chance we have of finding solutions."

As they dived down slowly through the blue-green water, Bianca was side-by-side with Maria, her diving buddy. Maria looked at her and used hand signals to ask: "Are you okay?"

"I am okay," Bianca signalled back.

Maria had given Bianca a small underwater camera to take photos of the aquatic life. Bianca swam alongside Maria, who was busy snapping photos.

Bianca's eyes were drawn to the fish. There were so many of them. She took photo after photo. Bianca looked up and saw the sun shining down, bringing light through the slightly murky water. The sight was so beautiful. Nothing had prepared Bianca for the joy of diving on a coral reef.

Maria beckoned Bianca, and she followed. The coral was interesting. Bianca felt like she was in an underwater forest. She began to look at the coral Maria was photographing.

Bianca was surprised to see a big patch of white on a large ball of purple coral. She also saw bands of white bleaching on orange and red and green coral. Some of the coral was completely white. As she took photos, her heart sank.

Back at the house, Bianca and Maria sat on the porch, drinking fruit juice and watching the sunset.

"Did you enjoy the dive?" Maria asked.

Bianca had so many different emotions running through her. She hugged Maria and didn't feel like letting go anytime soon. Bianca was usually shy, but she felt connected to Maria, the type of bond she had been missing since her mother died.

"When I was a little girl, the water was much clearer. Now, we have a lot of pollution," Maria said, looking out at the sunset. "There is lots of seaweed. It grows when there are too many nutrients in the water and it smothers the coral."

"How do the nutrients get into the water?"

Maria looked sad. "Pollution. The fertilisers that are used on farms get into the river, which flows into the ocean. And along the coast, all sorts of waste is flowing into the sea."

"Yuck!"

"I know, but scientists are working with communities. People are becoming more aware and coming up with solutions that can help make a difference. We all need to work together."

"That's a relief," said Bianca.

Eventually, the dark sky swallowed up the light. Bianca kept thinking about how everything was so interconnected.

What happens in one place, for better or worse, spreads to another.

Chapter 4
Separated

The next day, Maria took Bianca out again with her crew. Underwater, they saw a huge turtle and began taking photos. Then a large school of butterflyfish darted past. Bianca wanted to get that perfect shot. Maria had been impressed by her photos.

"You have an eye for composition. You capture the most powerful images." Bianca's heart leapt when Maria praised her talent. *At last someone appreciates me!*

Bianca followed the butterflyfish on and on, until she saw brightly coloured coral that reminded her of reindeer antlers. Royal blue and lime-green coral were growing like tentacles. There were no patches of white anywhere. She took photo after photo. She turned to see if Maria was as amazed by this beautiful coral as she was.

Where was Maria?

As Bianca swam about looking for Maria, she felt a rising sense of panic. After a few minutes, she came to a halt.

I might be swimming further away from Maria.

Bianca hung suspended in the water. *What am I going to do?* She felt small and helpless and she wanted to cry. She remembered feeling this way once before, on a day long ago. It was the day that Dad had sat her on his knee and told her, "Mum will not be coming home."

I am lost underwater. How could I be so stupid?
Bianca scolded herself. She felt as if she were shrinking and might disappear entirely when a submerged memory popped to the surface and flooded her mind. Bianca remembered her mum's smiling face. The memory calmed her.

Do not panic! Nothing good comes from panic!
Bianca tried to slow down her breathing and she thought about her training. She knew what to do. She'd been paying attention in diving training!

If I am separated from the others for more than two minutes, I should surface.

Bianca felt a surge of confidence. Now she had a plan. She took her small computer out of the pocket of her diving jacket and checked her depth – eight metres. She looked up to check that the way was clear above her, and made her way slowly upwards.

When she surfaced, Bianca quickly pressed the button on her buoyancy control device. Her jacket inflated as water slapped her face. The ocean had become very choppy.

Where's the boat?

Bianca looked around, to the right and to the left. No boat. Her diving gear was uncomfortable. It tipped her backwards. She felt like a turtle some mean person had upended in the sand.

Bianca's heart raced. What was she going to do? She still had her breathing regulator in her mouth, but as water splashed her face over and over, her chest tightened and she almost forgot how to breathe.

She looked above at a patch of blue sky. *Slow down.*

As she took control of her breathing, it occurred to Bianca the boat might be behind her. She turned. In the distance, between the waves, she saw the boat. But could they see her?

Bianca lifted her mask to rest on her head so the crew would know she was in trouble. She removed the breathing regulator from her mouth and waved her arm.

"Help!" she screamed, but her shout was pushed back towards her by the wind. Rough water pushed Bianca further from the boat. She put the breathing regulator back in her mouth.

They can't hear me. They might not even see me in this gigantic washing machine. It's up to me now.

Bianca remembered her training. She knew that if she fully inflated her diving jacket and turned on her back, she would stay afloat. She used her fins to splash and kick. She started to kick her way towards the boat.

It was Bianca's cousin Antonio who saw her.

"Bianca!" he called as he stood up in the boat. Bianca kicked as hard as she could with her strong legs. Her fins helped power her through the choppy waves.

Antonio and Maria pulled Bianca aboard. The diving team had surfaced when they were unable to find Bianca underwater. They'd been putting together a plan of action.

"Bianca! Bianca!" Maria said as she held her close. When Bianca told them how far she'd swam, they were impressed. "You've shown some good skills," said Antonio.

Bianca was exhausted. Her wetsuit was light, and now her body felt cold. She shivered. Maria wrapped her in a blanket and held her close all the way back to shore.

Bianca felt oddly calm. To distract herself, she showed Maria her underwater photos.

"You take very good photos," said Maria. "That coral that you saw is heat-resistant coral. It can cope with the rising sea temperatures. It's been grown in our nurseries and was transplanted to the reef a few years ago."

"That's good!"

"It's great," Maria said, and wrapped her arms tighter around Bianca. She sounded sad. "It's great, but it's not the coral I care about right now. I should have been with you. I am so glad you're safe."

When they got back to the house, Dad's face went white – and he was very quiet when Maria told him what had happened.

"It's my fault. I should have kept a better eye on her," said Maria. "It took me too long to notice she was missing."

Dad looked at Bianca, and she saw the disappointment in his eyes. *I've let Dad down,* Bianca thought.

"Bianca made a perfect ascent and showed strong survival skills swimming back to the boat," said Maria.

Bianca smiled, but Dad walked away. She heard a door slam shut. He was angry.

That night, Bianca and Dad sat on the porch and watched the sunset. "I could have lost you," Dad whispered.

Bianca thought he was being overly dramatic. "Maria says we were both at fault."

"No! If you can't take responsibility, maybe scuba diving is not the sport for a child."

Dad's words cut like a knife.

Bianca could barely hold back tears. "It will not happen again," she said, "I promise. I know there are diving rules for a reason. One minute I was with Maria. The next minute she was gone."

"No. You were gone!"

"I understand why you're mad at me."

"I'm not mad at you. I'm worried."

"Dad, I was so scared. Then I remembered Mum's face. It calmed me and I thought about my diving training. It helped me this afternoon."

Dad hugged her. "I just hope you have learnt a lesson."

"I have."

Chapter 5
A final dive

"Bianca, we have some staghorn coral from our nursery we're going to transplant onto the reef today. Would you like to help?" Maria asked at breakfast.

After what had happened the day before, Bianca could hardly believe she was being asked to join the team. She looked at her dad as inside she screamed, *Please let me go!*

Dad's face looked serious, but he said, "It's a good day for diving."

Dad is letting me go! As Bianca got her diving gear ready, she felt like the universe was smiling on her.

Bianca videoed Maria at work. On a barren part of the reef floor, Maria scraped a small patch clean. Then she took a blob of something that looked like putty and attached it to that patch. Maria then stuck a small piece of staghorn coral into the putty-like mixture. The first piece of coral had been transplanted!

Now, it was Bianca's turn. Maria showed her where to scrape and videoed Bianca as she worked.

The team planted pieces of coral for half an hour. Before they all surfaced, Maria measured the staghorn coral the team had planted last year. The coral was doing well and had spread across the reef floor. Maria and her team were making a difference.

This is the best job ever! thought Bianca.

Back at home in Auckland, Bianca sipped a mug of hot chocolate and peered through the glass at the butterflyfish. She smiled as she completed her homework for school.

Name someone who inspires you.

Maria, my cousin

Why does this person inspire you?

Maria is a marine biologist. She's part of a team of scientists who are working hard to save life on the Great Barrier Reef.

List three ways this person makes a difference in your life.

Maria trusts me. She makes me feel like I can do anything.

I am excited by the important work that Maria is doing.

I want to be a marine biologist like Maria.

"How's your homework going?" Dad asked.

"Great," said Bianca. She handed him the homework to read.

"Do you really want to be a marine biologist? It will involve a lot of study," Dad said.

"I know. I want to help these guys," she said, looking at the fish.

Dad laughed. "Bianca, I am so proud of you. I can't wait to see all the wonderful things you'll do when you grow up . . . but I don't have to wait that long. Let's go diving on the weekend."

"Yes!" said Bianca.

As she hugged Dad, Bianca pictured the butterflyfish swimming among the bright corals in the reef.

Soon, she promised, *I'll be out there helping you.*

A note
from the author

Sometimes I have trouble falling asleep at night, so I let my imagination take me on a journey. I glide through the water above brightly coloured coral and watch the brilliant fish as they dart away.

But I've never been scuba diving. When I was doing research to write *Colourful Coral,* I visited a diving centre. I wanted to see the diving gear Bianca would need, and I had many questions. I came away with lots of information and an enrolment form to learn scuba diving.